REMOTE LEARNING:

60 STRATEGIES

FOR SUCCESS

Helping Students Thrive in an Online Environment

Dr. Carrie Champ Morera

Decoding Telehealth

DEDICATION

In memory of my mother, Susan Champ.

CONTENTS

ACKNOWLEDGMENTS

It was important to me to obtain feedback from parents, school professionals, and technology professionals. They are all experts and offered their unique perspective on this topic. I would like to thank the following individuals for their review of this book:

Karetha C. (Maryland)
Dave Morera (Florida)
Sarah (Florida)

There were also three reviewers from New Jersey, Pennsylvania, and Texas who wish to remain anonymous.

Special thanks to Kristy Phillips, my amazing editor, and Angie Ayala, my talented cover designer, on this project.

1 INTRODUCTION

COVID-19 has disrupted our educational system. School staff have had to change the way they teach. Families have had to change their schedules and be more involved than ever in helping with their children's school tasks.

It's challenging for everyone! But we're in this together.

I wrote this book to help families with school-age children (grade 1 through high school) navigate the remote learning environment. I've seen and experienced how challenging eLearning can be, both as a psychologist working with children and families, and as a parent of distance learners. Almost 60% of parents of primary-school students and about half of parents of secondary-school students report that it's difficult to support their children's learning at home (Andrew, Cattan, Costa-Dias, Farquharson, Kraftman, Krutikove, Phimister, and Sevilla, 2020).

While remote learning may be new to millions of families, it's not a novel concept. In fact, virtual learning has been around for years. In my role as an independent school psychologist, I completed psychoeducational and psychological evaluations on remote learners even before the pandemic. They had many of the same challenges that remote learners are facing today.

Families and educators thrust into this alternative way of learning are discovering that it may be an opportunity to embrace online learning and continue down this path. We'll continue to see more eLearning in college, so having a solid remote-learning foundation will increase students' chances of success in the future. The in-person environment will likely remain the main learning method for some time. But we'll probably continue to see an increase in hybrid models, in which students split their time between online and in-person classrooms.

Whether your child is a distance learner, hybrid learner, or in-person learner, there's something for all families in this book. If learning at a distance is already going well for you, that's amazing, because it's not easy. I hope you'll find additional strategies in this book that help you make distance learning even better.

If eLearning has been a challenge and you're looking for tips to help your child be successful, this book is here to assist. Remote learning can be overwhelming and frustrating, but it doesn't have to stay that way. I want to help get you and your family to a place where it's manageable—and even enjoyable.

This book is filled with strategies designed to improve the remote learning experience. Read this book slowly. It's divided into sections so you can go back and re-read areas that apply to issues you're trying to resolve.

As you begin to think about what strategies you would like to try, I encourage you to start small. Take a couple of tips from this book and apply them to your situation. After you've used those strategies, come back to this book, then choose and apply a couple more. If you're feeling overwhelmed and not sure where to start, begin with the first strategy and build from there.

While these strategies may be helpful for all school-age children, you might use them differently for a first-grader than you would for a seventh-grader. If you have younger children, you'll need to take the lead (and in some cases full responsibility) for using these strategies. And you may have to continue being a part of them. Younger children may not be ready to independently use and stick with these ideas. They can learn them, but they'll need regular reinforcement and practice. Be patient.

If your child is going to school in person or participating in eLearning only temporarily, I hope you find a few tips here that you can apply when your child is at home completing homework or missed school and needs to complete assignments and projects at home. You'll find that some of these strategies, if used correctly, will help build a foundation for achieving other personal and professional goals.

Finally, the strategies in this book are not an exhaustive list. Some families may have developed others that work for them. (I would love to hear about them!) While the strategies I share are a starting point, you may need a deeper dive into specific strategies depending on your family's situation. For example, children with learning disabilities, physical disabilities, and mental health concerns may need more strategies.

I hope that each family will find some tips that will make a positive difference for them. The important thing to remember is that the goal is to have a healthy learning environment that allows your child to feel confident, enjoy learning, develop socially, and make academic progress.

2 HOW THIS BOOK WILL HELP YOU

Take a look at your child's current learning situation to determine the strengths and challenges in your family. This will give you a starting point for improvements.

Before reading any further, ask yourself these questions:

- What is going well with remote learning?
- What challenges is my child having?
- What concerns do I have about my child's school performance, behavior, social skills, and mental health?
- How have I tried to address these concerns and challenges?
- What does success look like for my child in a remote learning environment?

This book will show you how to:

- Set up and maintain an eLearning space that encourages learning
- Apply strategies keep your child engaged
- Understand the emotional impact of eLearning and how to support and motivate your child
- Find ways to motivate your child to learn
- Understand the importance of home-school communication
- Identify what you can do for yourself to help your child succeed

3 TERMINOLOGY

Before we get into tips and strategies, let's cover terminology for learning at a distance—or, learning that physically occurs in a location outside the traditional brick-and-mortar school. This terminology varies from country to state to region to city.

Learning at a distance explained

The following terms are names for learning at a distance:

- Remote learning
- eLearning
- Virtual learning
- Online learning
- Cyberschool
- Home learning
- Distance learning
- Distance education

These terms may be used interchangeably, but I'll use *eLearning* and *remote learning* most frequently. In this book, the terms *parents* and *caregivers* are also used interchangeably because it's not always the parent who is the caregiver. Sometimes a grandparent, other relative, or friend is in this role.

4 IMPORTANCE OF EXPECTATIONS AND ROUTINES

Successful distance learning begins with a solid foundation. Children look to adults to model how to behave, particularly during stressful events and when they feel uncertain about what to do next. They rely on guidance from adults to help them make decisions and develop the skills they need to make good choices in the future and become responsible adults.

When you send your child to school (in the brick-and-mortar building), you expect school staff to establish and follow through with expectations for academic and classroom behavior. This takes effort, time, attention, and consistency. So, it's unrealistic for caregivers to set up their children at a workspace and expect them to attend class and complete their schoolwork without laying the groundwork first. Simply making technology available to students doesn't automatically translate into self-directed learning (Sieber, 2005). Caregivers, in partnership with the school, need to establish expectations and routines.

Routines will keep you and your family organized, and that will provide a structure around distance learning. Routines provide stability, predictability, and a sense of control. They also contribute to improved well-being and support child development (Spagnola & Fiese, 2007). When you establish and maintain a daily routine, it lets children know what to expect and what's expected of them. Plus, it provides them with a way to cope with other stressors.

When you set your child's daily routine for each part of the day, keep these tips in mind:

School mornings

- Set a consistent time for wake-up.
- Be positive and pleasant in the morning with your children (even if it's challenging).
- Complete hygiene tasks (bathroom activities, getting dressed).
- Eat breakfast.
- Say goodbye to family members or exchange kind words before you start the day.

After school and evenings

- If a responsible adult isn't in the home at the time, check in on your child or have another adult check in.
- Have your child complete homework, then enjoy afterschool activities, exercise, rest, free time.
- Eat dinner together as a family (when possible) without technology distractions. Talk about your day. And avoid negative comments at the dinner table!
- Children can help with dinner activities (prepare, cook, or clean up).
- Complete chores (at this time or other assigned time of day or day of the week).

Bedtime

- Get materials ready for school for the next day.
- Choose clothes for the morning.
- Complete hygiene tasks (wash face/shower, brush teeth, pajamas).
- Establish and follow nighttime rituals (reading, conversation, relaxing music). Engage in only calm

activities, and no electronics.
- Set a time for lights-out, and follow it.
- Don't let your child keep smartphones and other handheld electronic devices in the bedroom. They can be tempting to use during the night. Get in the habit of storing them in a common area overnight while they're being charged.

Weekends

- Family time: games, outings, activities, togetherness.
- Alone time: rest time, thinking time, solitary activities.
- Social time: connecting with peers.
- While weekends can have more flexibility, such as waking up later and going to bed later, don't throw all structure out the window.

Start building a foundation now for your child. It's never too late! Keep in mind that you may get some resistance from family members as you try to establish routines, particularly if they aren't used to them. Be persistent. If you already have routines for your child, what areas can be improved? Incorporate the tips and strategies in this book into a daily routine.

Finally, the daily and remote learning routine that you and your family establish will likely look different from another family's routine. That's okay as long as it works for you and your family. Each family has its own challenges.

Routines can be tough to establish, and they won't go as expected 100% of the time. Things come up that we can't plan for! You may need to adjust routines from time to time when something doesn't work. Stay consistent and continue to expect your children to stick to routines.

While all children benefit from routines, expectations depend on the child's age. For example, younger children rely more heavily on their caregivers to complete parts of the daily routine. Teach your children along the way. The older your children become, the more independent they'll be if they have practice and good role models.

5 SIX KEY AREAS FOR SUCCESSFUL eLEARNING

What are the six key areas for success in remote learning?

1. **Physical environment**

This is the physical set-up, including equipment, supplies, and room location. What does the learning environment look like at your house?

2. **eLearning considerations**

This includes things your child needs to do to be successful. How can your child learn best?

3. **Emotional considerations**

Think about your child's emotional state and needs. How is eLearning impacting your child? What can you do to help?

4. **Motivational strategies**
Find out what you can do to keep your child motivated and engaged in online schooling. How can you give an extra push?

5. **Home-school communication**

Good communication between the home and school are important

REMOTE LEARNING: 60 STRATEGIES FOR SUCCESS

for success. How can you work better with your child's school?

6. Caregiver's role

You play an important part in getting your eLearner on the right track. What do you need to do for yourself and your child?

All of these parts work together. And all parts play a role in your child's eLearning success. As you read this book, think about which areas are strengths for you and your child and which areas could use some attention.

Six Key Areas for Success in an eLearning Environment

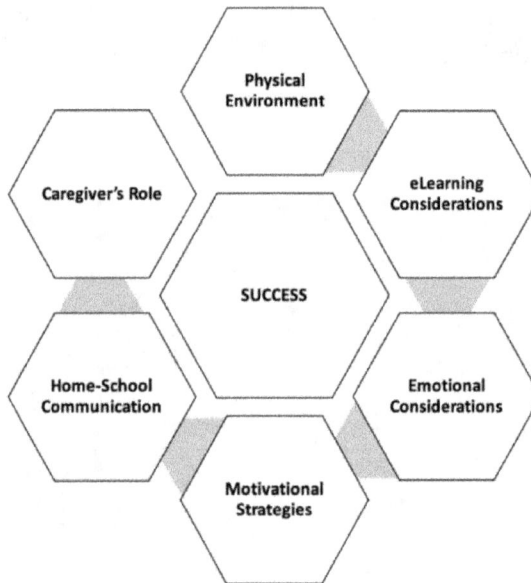

6 PHYSICAL ENVIRONMENT

The first key area for successful eLearning is the physical environment. This is your set-up, including equipment, supplies, and room location.

What does the learning environment look like at your house?

1. Find the space in your home that's right for learning.

Location, location, location.

It's ideal to have a separate room dedicated to eLearning and work activities. That will help maintain a physical and mental separation between home and school. An unused room or closet will work.

However, not every family will have space for this. If you don't have a whole room available, pick a space you can dedicate to school. This could be a corner of almost any room. If space is at a premium and you don't have space just for eLearning, find a table or desk that you can use regularly. Make that your child's workspace. At the end of each day, have them put all their school materials in a box so you can also use that space for other home activities.

Try to avoid using areas that are noisy or busy during school time. But your child may want a location with some background noise, similar to what they hear in a traditional classroom.

You might have to experiment with spaces. If one doesn't work for your child, explore another spot.

If you have a young child or a child with attention difficulties, it's helpful to sit close to your child so you can monitor their eLearning. These children struggle to focus and will need to be directed.

If possible, avoid setting up the eLearning environment in your child's bedroom or wherever they sleep. That space should be for relaxation and rest. When we're constantly working in the area where we sleep, our brain starts to think we're in a place of work. So, you'll strengthen your child's mental association between their bedroom and sleeping when you move computers, TVs, and work materials out of that space.

If your child must have their distance learning set up in their room due to space limitations or privacy needs, follow these simple guidelines:

- Avoid doing any schoolwork on the bed.

- Keep the eLearning workspace separate from the rest of the room.

- Use the eLearning workspace for schoolwork only.

- Put up a divider between the workspace and the rest of the room.

2. Select the proper equipment.

Equipment to consider:

- Learning device

- Webcam

- Speakers and microphone

- Headphones with built-in microphone

- Printer

- Wireless equipment

- Power strip with USB ports

Learning device

Children spend about five hours a day on average on remote learning, so they need an appropriate learning device (Andrew, Cattan, Costa-Dias, Farqharson, Kraftman, Krtikova, Phimister, Sevilla, 2020). Use a desktop computer, laptop, or standard-size tablet. Smartphones and iPad Minis aren't ideal for completing most schoolwork.

Webcam

Not all computers come with webcams. But a webcam is a great option if you're looking to enhance the online learning experience. Some brands, such as Logitech, offer widescreen video and even automatically correct lighting for a crisper video. If yours comes with a universal clip, you can use it to easily attach the webcam to your screen.

Speakers and microphone

Not all computers come with quality speakers or a microphone. At high volumes, factory components can pop and crackle, greatly diminishing the sound quality. For online lessons, you need clean, crisp audio. There are speakers and microphones that you can plug into a USB port. Bluetooth speakers and microphones are great wireless options. During independent learning, students can also use the speakers to review their lessons.

Headphones with built-in microphone

Headphones help block outside sound and are ideal for listening to class instruction. If your child uses standard earphones or the computer speaker, the class may hear you and other family members talking in the background. But if your child's headphones or earphones have a built-in microphone, the headphone's mic will be very close to your child's mouth and won't pick up background sounds. This setup is ideal for receiving calls and participating in live class sessions. After using headphones for a while, your child's ears may hurt, so having the external speakers and a microphone as an option allows your child to switch back and forth.

Printer

Most teachers make a home printer optional. However, having one allows your child to print out worksheets that could be more difficult to complete online. It also provides a break from the screen and an opportunity to exercise fine-motor skills through writing. And your child may want to study in paper form or print and display a completed project.

Wireless equipment

Your child's remote education experience hinges on your Wi-Fi connection. Being booted from a lesson can make it hard for your student to be engaged and retain what they're learning. So you may need to upgrade your home network.

If your Wi-Fi signal is weak, a Wi-Fi extender may help. These devices boost your existing router signal around the house. This can help shore up the signal in parts of the home with bad connections.

If your wireless equipment is old, or if the signal is strong and you're still having connectivity issues, check to see if your current wireless standard (e.g., 802.11ac) supports high speeds and multiple connections. If it doesn't, you may need to upgrade the router. If the router has a wireless integrated access point and doesn't support the newer standards, call your internet provider for help.

Power strip with USB ports

Many students need to use several devices, often at the same time.

Many newer laptops have few, if any, ports to help with external recharges. Running all of these devices off the laptop can quickly drain its battery midway through the school day. A power strip with USB ports is a convenient way to keep all your devices fully charged without burying your laptop under a mountain of cables. Keep laptops plugged in when stationed near an outlet.

3. Select an appropriate seat and position for learning.

Posture

In order to be productive, your child needs to sit properly. That means sitting upright with feet flat on the floor and shoulders back. To reduce back strain, they should recline slightly back at a 110- to 130-degree angle from their desk. If their feet don't reach the floor, use a footrest. Arms should be parallel to the floor when using the keyboard. Make sure your child's head is straight, and remind them to avoid slouching. Poor posture can lead to biased memories, headaches, and digital eyestrain. It can also decrease your child's interest in learning, even during the most interesting lessons (Castellucci, Arezes, & Molenbroek, 2015).

Did you know that sitting straight can help you think positively and improve your mood? (Wison & Peper, 2004). This will allow you to get more work done.

Seating options

High-back chairs and adjustable armchairs are good ergonomic options. Chairs with gas pumps and side levers let you change the height of the seat and positioning of the backrest so your child can work without spinal strain.

Positioning the screen

Position the screen 20 to 30 inches from your child's face and make sure their eyes are level with the very top of the monitor. If the screen needs to be higher but you can't adjust it, stack some hardcover books beneath it. Raising or lowering the chair can also help. Your child should be looking slightly down at schoolwork. The center of the screen should be between 15 and 20 degrees below horizontal eye level.

Seating considerations

Regardless of the seat you select, make sure your child leaves it between classes and during other breaks. If they work for extended periods, they should stand up every 30 minutes. This can help energize them. Standing desks are another option if your child has difficulty sitting still or feels fatigued from sitting too long.

4. Have the right school materials.

Check your child's school schedule for the upcoming week and make sure you have everything they need at the workspace, ready to go. Include back-up supplies so your child doesn't run out.

Suggested school materials:

- Pencils
- Pens
- Erasers
- Notebooks
- Post-it Notes
- Binders
- Stapler
- Glue
- Tape
- Scissors
- Highlighters
- Crayons
- Markers

A supply box like the one your child would use in the classroom is helpful.

5. Organize the environment to optimize success.

Now that you have all the right materials, it's time to get organized.

An organized workspace will help your student be more productive. Make sure the workspace is clean and neat. Include only the needed devices, materials, and supplies in the workspace. That means no toys, projects, and other objects! Use a pencil holder, school supply box, or bin to keep everything in.

If the workspace is near the wall, you can hang up a calendar, bulletin board, or schedule. Record due dates and important school events, then review the information at the start of each school day.

Consider having your child help organize the learning environment. You can provide all the materials then work together to set everything up. This will help your child become more interested in remote learning and give them a sense of ownership in the space.

Putting extra time into organizing a workspace will help your child be prepared for class. They'll have everything they need handy (if everything is kept there) and won't have to run around the house to find supplies at the start of class.

If you have more than one child, and space and devices are limited, children may need to share the workspace and resources. In these cases, schedule times for children to use the designated space and device.

6. Remove distractions.

Anything that regularly diverts your child's attention from schoolwork is considered a distraction!

- **No smartphones**
- **No extra devices**
- **No additional materials**
- **No TV or videogames**
- **No noisy appliances running in the background**

Remove all distractions so that your house is like the classroom environment. In a recent study, middle school, high school, and college students who were observed studying averaged less than six minutes on an academic task prior to being distracted by technology, such as social media, texting, and a preference for switching tasks (Rosen, Carrier, & Cheever, 2013). It would be challenging to study and complete assignments with these interruptions and distractions!

Older students may own smartphones. However, if they're doing their work on a laptop or desktop, they don't need their phone while they're learning. Instead of just turning the device off, consider keeping it in another room or holding on to it while your child is in class. This will help your child not feel compelled to frequently check their phone.

If there are TVs, stereos, video games, devices, or anything else in the room that makes noise, turn them off and don't have the remote controls nearby. Try not to have dishwashers, vacuums, or washing machines running. And make sure no one is listening to or playing music during eLearning time.

7. Dress for success.

Teach your child how to dress for success. This doesn't necessarily mean they need to wear a dress or suit and tie for school. But do encourage them to wear something other than what they slept in as a first step in getting ready for the day. Clothes should be appropriate for the situation. Anything clean and comfortable should work just fine.

But that doesn't mean your child should wear pajamas for eLearning! After all, they wouldn't wear pajamas to in-person school (unless it was pajama day). Pajamas shouldn't be an all-day thing, and wearing them for school on a daily basis can make your child feel lazy and sluggish. It can also disrupt their internal biological clock and lead to sleep problems, moodiness, and low energy. In fact, in a recent study, 52% of students reported that clothing has an influence on learning effectiveness (Naddeo, Califano, & Fiorillo, 2021).

Children thrive on structure and routine; this includes having a regular bedtime and wake-up time. Routines help reduce anxiety and lead to overall better mental health. Good first steps for each day are to have your child put on fresh clothes, brush their teeth, comb their hair, wash their face, and eat breakfast. If they didn't take a shower the night before, they should take one before school starts. When your child pays attention to their hygiene routine in the morning, it helps get them in the learning mode, both physically and mentally.

If your child is slow to get going in the morning, lay out clothes the night before. This saves time in the morning and can reduce parent-child battles about what to wear.

8. Keep a water bottle at the workspace.

Water is the healthiest drink. It helps the body and brain stay hydrated, reduces fatigue, and can prevent headaches. It also improves motivation, concentration, and overall brain function. Besides, it's refreshing and helps keep you alert.

How much water should your school-age child drink?

> **5-8 years:** 7 cups
> **7-13 years:** 9 to 10 cups
> **14+ years:** 10 to 14 cups
> **Children who are active will need to drink more water (NIH, n.d.).**

It's important to stay hydrated throughout the day. So have your child keep a filled water bottle at their workspace. Having their drink handy means they won't need to step away from the learning environment to get a drink in the middle of class. Similarly, children often keep water bottles at their desks in the school building, so it's a good idea to do the same at home.

What if your child doesn't like water? Add flavor! Lemons, oranges, berries, cherries, watermelon, cucumbers, and mint are all great ways to make water tasty and still healthy. Plus, adding variety may encourage your child to drink more of it. For example, seltzer water or sparkling water has bubbles in it, and many children think it's fun to drink. However, avoid enhancers that include artificial sweeteners (like Sucralose and sucrose acetate isobutyrate), colorings, and additives (like propylene glycol, which is in antifreeze).

9. Keep devices and materials for eLearning separate from recreational use.

If you have multiple laptops, desktops, tablets, or other devices, reserve some for educational use only and keep them in your child's workspace. That way, the workspace will be ready to go each day. This will prevent assignments from getting lost or unintentionally altered or deleted. This also makes it less likely that the devices will be broken or lost.

If you need to share learning devices with the household or for recreational use, follow these tips:

- Create a separate profile for each purpose and person. That way, when "Child1-School" logs in, they see one view that has their school information and applications. Then, when "Child1-Home" logs in, they see their games and social apps.

- During recreational use, don't change educational settings or use the apps and websites dedicated for remote use.

- Leave device settings for educational use in place.

- Each night, return the devices to the learning space.

- Charge the device in the learning space.

10. Print materials, if necessary.

Printed material is portable, and children can read it when and where they like. So some students prefer to have information on paper in front of them like they do when they're in an in-person class.

Many children remember information better when they can read and study it in their hands. They can take notes and highlight the text if they want. Yes, children can use these tools on the screen if the learning platform allows it, but not all children like this method. At the very least, printing a few pages from a lesson can be helpful.

Also, if working directly on the screen, such as an online worksheet, is a challenge, talk to your child's teacher to see if you can print it instead, complete it, and then upload it for grading.

Having a printer could be beneficial, as your child may have work they simply can't complete online. Doing work on paper also gives your child a break from the screen. If you don't have a printer, arrange with the school to get work that needs to be on paper.

Research suggests that student preference is associated with achievement (Chang & Ley, 2006). In other words, students who wanted printed materials and had access to them were more likely to do well. So take your child's learning preferences into account, if possible, when there's an option to print what they need.

11. Wear blue light glasses or use a screen protector.

Some children may complain that their eyes bother them from looking at the screen for long periods. Their eyes may feel tired, sore, or watery. They may have eyestrain, neck/shoulder pain, and headaches. Computer vision syndrome (CVS) is an umbrella term for symptoms often associated with extended screen time.

To alleviate these symptoms, try adjusting the lighting on your child's device. Taking screen breaks, using a matte screen filter to reduce glare, and using artificial tears when your child's eyes feel dry can be helpful. But if the problem persists, it may be at least partially due to blue light.

Blue light glasses reportedly block some of the blue light that screens give off. Some people who used them have reported less eyestrain and say they can see screen images more easily. Blue light glasses may help resolve some symptoms of CVS, but more research is needed (Dabrowiecki, Villalobos, & Krupinski, 2020).

You could also apply a blue light film to the screen. Blue light filtering screen protectors use a special coating that blocks light in the 380-to-500-nanometer range.

Electronics like phones that use LED or OLED panels emit blue light to help brightness and improve clarity, but that light can also reach the rear of the retina. As a result, blue light can increase alertness. But it also can make it difficult to sleep. That's because exposure to blue light suppresses the body's production of sleep-inducing melatonin.

If your student keeps having eye problems as a result of remote learning, make sure they've had a recent eye exam to rule out other vision issues, such as nearsightedness, farsightedness, or accommodative dysfunction.

Accommodative dysfunction is an eye-focusing problem that causes blurred vision—up close and/or far away. It's often found in children who spend long periods of time focusing on work that is close to them. Prescription glasses and/or vision therapy is the usual treatment.

12. Adjust the contrast, text, and color settings on the screen for comfort.

Lighting is important. Your child shouldn't work in the dark or stare at the sun or other light source. Make sure their workspace has adequate light.

You want their monitor's brightness to match the brightness of the surrounding workspace. To achieve this, look at the white background on this page. If it looks like a light source in the room, it's too bright. If it seems dull and gray, it's probably too dark.

Also consider text and color. Text should be three times the smallest size you can read from a normal viewing position—which is 20 to 30 inches from the monitor. When it comes to color combinations, the eyes prefer black text on a white or slightly yellow background. Other dark-on-light combinations work fine for most people. Avoid low-contrast text/background color schemes.

Make adjustments until you find the most comfortable settings for your child.

13. Test the learning platform and technology before class begins.

Technology and learning platforms

Get familiar with the devices and website your child will use for remote learning. Technology frequently changes, so it can be a challenge to keep up with the applications and features. If you struggle with technology, reach out to your child's school first, as they may have instructions and video tutorials that could help you.

At the start of each day

Prepare, prepare, prepare! Make sure your child is able to log in to the learning platform and any other websites they need for the week. That way, if your child has trouble, you'll have time to troubleshoot and fix any issues. Make sure you have the correct school contact for technical support.

Before each class

Have your child log in to each class several minutes early just in case there are delays or connection problems. That way, they won't miss anything important at the beginning of class. And make sure your child has each teacher's contact information as well as a technical support contact handy.

14. Plan each Sunday for the week ahead.

If you fail to plan, then you are planning to fail.

Make it a habit to plan for school each week. For example, each Sunday night spend 10 to 15 minutes with your child reviewing the schedule for the upcoming week.

Does your child have all the supplies they need? Make sure they're easily in reach.

What assignments and projects are due for the week? Make notes on a calendar or planner.

Does your child like having a printed weekly schedule? If so, print it and post it in their workspace.

When will your child take breaks and eat lunch? Prepare snacks and meals ahead of time.

Consider anything else that may impact the upcoming week, such as family plans or extracurricular activities. Planning helps reduce your child's anxiety and improves their confidence because they know what to do and what to expect.

We've covered the physical aspects of eLearning. Now you have your supplies, equipment, desk, chair, and electronic devices. Most importantly, you have a dedicated space for your child to work in. In the next section, we'll cover how to successfully navigate the distance learning environment.

7 eLEARNING CONSIDERATIONS

The second key to success is focusing on what occurs during eLearning. This includes everything students should be doing during their school day to maximize success. How can your child learn best?

1. Use a high-speed internet connection.

What is high-speed internet and why do you need it?

Internet speed is the speed at which data can move through an internet connection. If you have high-speed internet at home, eLearning will go much more smoothly.

Speed is measured in megabits per second, or Mbps.

100 Mbps or higher: This can handle multiple online activities for multiple users at once without interruptions or slowdowns.

100 to 200 Mbps: This can handle streaming and video chat for up to five users at once.

200 to 1,000 Mbps: This is faster than average and can easily support multiple users at once.

How to check your home internet speed:

1. Connect your computer to your router using an Ethernet cable.
2. Connect to the internet.
3. Open your web browser.
4. Navigate to www.speedtest.net.
5. Tap **Go**.
6. If your internet speed isn't good based on the descriptions above, contact your internet provider for options.

2. Minimize the use of Wi-Fi and consider hard-wiring.

To avoid interruptions and slowdowns, have others in the home minimize their use of Wi-Fi, including services that take up a lot of bandwidth, such as streaming video, while your child is eLearning.

If you have multiple children doing eLearning and/or you're also working from home, consider hard-wiring via an Ethernet cable for internet access. This gives you the fastest and most stable connection. A hard-wired Ethernet connection is certainly the better option if you have a designated workspace for the device your child is using for remote learning.

Putting all of your computers and devices on Wi-Fi can slow things down for everyone. If you use Wi-Fi, you'll need to wait for Wi-Fi signals, which may go in and out or be weak in certain areas of your home. You can lose time and productivity while waiting on a slow Wi-Fi connection.

The benefits of using a wired Ethernet connection:
- **Reduced demand on Wi-Fi:** Remove some devices from Wi-Fi to reduce the demand on your wireless router and improve devices that need it.
- **Faster connection speed:** Hard-wired connections can be up to five times faster than Wi-Fi.
- **Reliable connection:** Since the signal is wired directly to your computer, it doesn't have to travel through the air like Wi-Fi and risk interference from furniture and walls.
- **Lower latency:** This means webpages and educational apps load and respond faster.

3. Increase your network's security.

You don't want unauthorized users to have access to your child's eLearning materials, applications, and platforms. Network security helps protect your devices from harmful spyware. It also prevents hackers from stealing your data and gaining access to your email, programs, and systems (D. Morera, personal communication, February 23, 2021).

Follow these steps to increase network security:

1. Ensure your devices have the latest updates to protect you from hackers.
2. Ensure your router/Wi-Fi access points have the manufacturer's latest firmware.
3. Turn off features on your router that you don't need. This prevents unnecessary ports from being accessible outside your home network.
4. Use complex passwords and change them often.
5. Select the strongest Wi-Fi security protocol that your router supports. For example, WPA-2PSK is stronger than WPA and WEP.
6. Use antivirus software.
7. Don't open links from unfamiliar websites or emails. Attackers use them to install malware, viruses, and ransomware.
8. Create a separate profile for your child that doesn't have system privileges and prevents them from installing unwanted software.

4. Mimic a classroom setting by mirroring the screen to a TV.

Mirroring is when you send the content from a computer, laptop, smartphone, or tablet screen to a TV or another monitor via a cable or wireless connection.

Mirroring your child's device to a TV is a great way to bring the classroom to life in your home. You can replay videos, present slideshows, and experience the feeling of being in a classroom at home. Some children may find this more interactive because the screen is so big.

The mirroring process is quick and easy to do. However, instructions can vary depending on your device and TV. You'll need to research your options because there are too many to discuss in this book.

How well mirroring works depends how strong and reliable your Wi-Fi signal is and how powerful the device is. If you have trouble with Wi-Fi, try an HDMI cable or adapter (hard-wired option). If you're using an older TV, you may need other cables like a VGA or DVI.

5. Log out and close applications and programs you're not using.

It's always good to log out and close all applications and programs that aren't being used during online learning.

Why?

When other applications are open and running in the background, they consume resources and may fight for bandwidth. And that means remote live lessons and video streaming may be interrupted or disconnected. Bandwidth on each device is limited. So, unused open programs and applications may slow down the applications your child is using. It may also take longer for lessons and other learning materials to load

Additionally, notifications that pop up on the screen (like email, games, messages, or computer notifications) may distract your child. When unused programs and applications are closed, your child will likely not encounter these problems. That means they can better focus on the task at hand and not be pulled away by pop-ups and other interruptions.

The way you close applications and programs depends on your operating system and device. There are usually a few ways to do it.

Make sure your child opens only the platform and materials they need during class, because everything else is a distraction. The value of multitasking is a myth. The brain can't successfully handle the cognitive demands of multiple tasks simultaneously. For example, studying, homework, learning activities, and grades are all likely negatively affected when a student multitasks with technology (Carrier, Rosen, Cheever, & Lim, 2015). Learning suffers. So turn off those smartphones, TVs, and video games and take them out of the learning environment.

6. Adjust lighting in the room during instruction.

Room light levels are important because they allow your child to clearly see the information presented on the screen. They also let the teacher and classmates can see your child during instruction if they're on live video.

Follow these tips during eLearning (not on video):

- If possible, use a location with natural light.

- Avoid having direct sunlight behind your child. It causes a glare on the screen that makes it difficult to see the information being presented.

- Avoid direct sunlight in front of your child. It makes it hard to see what's in front of them.

- Make sure overhead lights and lamps are bright enough, but not so bright that they create a glare on the screen.

Follow these tips during video conferencing:

- Use a steady lamp, directly by your child's face, for even, consistent lighting.

- Don't use sidelights or backlights.

- Make sure your child avoids sitting with their back to the window (unless blinds or other window treatments are fully closed). Otherwise, the camera will expose the light and make your child appear as a silhouette.

7. Have your student look away and take a break from the workspace.

Your child is spending hours in front of the screen each day during remote learning. And that can cause fatigue, eyestrain, and muscle soreness. That's because their eyes are focused on a small area, whereas in the traditional classroom there's more opportunity to look around and move.

20-20-20 rule

It's not healthy to sit in one space, working and focusing on a screen for hours at a time. So teach your child to follow the 20-20-20 rule throughout the school day. That means looking away from the screen every 20 minutes for 20 seconds at a time and focusing on a fixed point 20 feet away.

Take breaks

If your child has time between classes, encourage them to get up and walk away from the workspace. And breaks shouldn't include screens! Healthy breaks include using the restroom, grabbing a snack, taking a brain break, talking to someone in the home, stretching, or doing jumping jacks.

Unfortunately, not all schools provide significant breaks or adjustment time between classes. But at the very least, children will have a chance to take their eyes off the screen for a moment, stand up, and stretch. Talk to school staff if your student doesn't get enough time to transition.

These strategies give your child's eyes some relief from looking at the screen and their body an opportunity to move. Playtime and downtime are crucial to well-being and learning.

8. Get outside or exercise during the day.

After doing schoolwork for hours, children should get up and get moving. In addition to regular physical education classes (if they have one), your child needs to take multiple breaks during the day. They should at least go outside for a few minutes and get some fresh air or go for a walk. If the weather is bad or it's not safe to go outside, find a small space in the home where they can stretch to loosen muscles and improve flexibility. They should also do cardio to improve overall health (they can do jumping jacks and burpees, run in place, and hop on one foot in the house). If your child wakes up early, they can exercise before they start their day. That's always a good time because exercise prior to working helps increase focus and productivity.

Our bodies are made to move. School-age children and teens should get 60 minutes or more of moderate to vigorous physical activity each day. So they should do several types of physical activity each week. Aerobic activities, such as walking, running, or anything that makes the heart beat faster, is important for healthy development. Second, muscle-strengthening activities, like climbing or pull-ups, help build strength. Finally, bone-strengthening activities, such as jumping or running, are important for flexibility and healthy bone development.

Exercise improves fitness, increases concentration, can improve academic performance, builds a healthy body, improves self-esteem, improves posture and balance, and encourages healthy growth and development. All children need time for play and exercise.

9. Eat lunch and snacks away from the workspace.

We discussed the importance of taking breaks. Lunch and nutritious snacks are essential, but children should eat in an area separate from where their schooling takes place. Even if the workspace is set up in the kitchen, they can still step away from their computer and go to another area in the kitchen to eat.

This isn't to say your child can never eat lunch or snacks in their workspace. Their class might have a celebration, or perhaps your child is in a virtual lunch group. If you have one device for remote learning and it's not easy to move it to another room for these kinds of situations, then your student will need to stay in their learning space. However, when possible, have them move to another location with their device for a change of scenery.

Be cautious of overeating and undereating. If children eat while they're working, they can begin to snack excessively and develop a habit of mindless eating. On the other hand, some children become overly focused on their work and forget to eat. They may even avoid eating to get more work done. So fix snacks ahead of time and plan a time for snack breaks at designated times. This gives your child something to look forward to and can motivate them to complete assignments.

10. Be accessible to your child as needed.

You know your child well. And each situation will be different. Generally, children around fourth grade and younger may need to be in a learning space that's close to a caregiver or responsible adult during eLearning. Someone may need to make sure that they're paying attention, have access to materials, and complete assignments. And you may need to be handy to troubleshoot any difficulties.

Older and more independent children may be successful in another room or area of the home with limited supervision. But they too may encounter difficulties and need your help. Even if your child is independent, it's still a good idea to check in on them. It lets them know you care. Plus, it emphasizes the importance of education. Let students of all ages know who (you or someone else) can help them if needed and the best way to contact that person.

For example, if you work from home, let your child know that if you're on a conference call or your door is closed, then they'll need to wait until the door is open to come in. If there are multiple caregivers in the home during remote learning, try to make sure one of you is available at all times. If you're not home during the day, arrange for another caregiver to check in on your child. Another option is to have a video call or phone call with your child. Texting can work too. Occasional check-ins are important, but you don't need to do it every ten minutes.

Each family's situation is different. Work out a system with your child and other adults who need to be involved. Make adjustments as necessary.

11. Follow a weekly schedule, even if classes are asynchronous.

The remote learning environment may look different from one school to the next. Some schools require eLearners to follow a bell schedule, moving from one class to the next at designated times. These students may need to sign in to class or attend live lessons. Their class and work schedules are typically set.

Other schools may have a list of assignments that are due for the day or week. It's up to the students to decide when and how to complete their work.

For children who have regularly scheduled live sessions, there may be times when class isn't live due to teacher absences, technology challenges, or schedule changes. When classes are not in real time, encourage your child to stay with their regular school routine and complete their work independently during scheduled time.

If your child has the flexibility to complete assignments on their own time, have them make a schedule they can follow each week. This provides structure and accountability. These strategies will allow your child to stay on track.

12. Provide a fidget toy or stress ball.

Have a fidget toy or stress ball available if one could help your child. While fidget toys or stress balls may be distracting to some children, it may help those who are anxious or need to move frequently. These materials can calm children and allow them to relax and focus during instruction. In a recent study, typically developing children were not distracted and completed tasks easily while using a fidget toy (Kirby, 2020).

What are fidget toys and stress balls?

A fidget toy is small object that you can push, pull, or squeeze. Some children focus better when their hands are in action. Examples of fidgets include kneaded erasers, ponytail holders, stress balls, squishy toys, and magnetic balls or discs.

A stress ball is a malleable toy that you squeeze to relieve muscle tension and stress.

The benefits of fidget toys and stress balls include:

- Improved learning benefits
- Less anxiety and stress
- Better dexterity
- Improved coordination and fine motor skills
- Help with the development of hand muscles
- Improved concentration and attention to tasks (by allowing the brain to filter out extrasensory information)

If you think your child needs a fidget toy or stress ball, provide it and monitor to make sure they're using it appropriately. Don't provide too many, as this will be distracting. Stick with one. If you want to switch it out for another one for the second half of the day or the next day, that could work too.

13. Have your student take notes during class.

Even if note-taking isn't required, it can help your child stay focused during class and remember more of what they learn. It will help them actively listen during instruction time and understand the course material. Notes will also serve as study material for tests and assignments.

Handwritten notes prompt children to think about what they're writing. This is missed when notes are typewritten. Taking notes with pen and paper helps internalize the information.

Handwriting helps strengthen the learning process. It gives the brain feedback from the child's hand movements. This feedback is different from what your child gets when typing on a keyboard. Handwriting leaves a motor memory in the sensorimotor part of the brain. This helps children recognize letters and make a strong connection between the writing and reading process.

However, some children do better typing than writing. Some struggle with spelling or the motor movements involved in writing. If this is the case for your child, you may want to consider having a second monitor. This way they can use the keyboard and type material on one screen and see the material being presented on the other. If you don't have a second monitor, you can split your main screen so your child can view and interact with multiple windows at the same time.

14. Use a study carrel or divider.

What is a study carrel or divider?

A study carrel can be a desk that has built-in partitions on the sides and back. It can be also be a separate piece with two sides and a back that you put on top of the desk or table where your child does schoolwork.

A divider is a partition, wall, or privacy screen that surrounds part of the child's working area and blocks it from another part of the room.

Why use a study carrel or divider?

They provide privacy and block out distractions. This is especially helpful for children who may get distracted easily or have difficulty concentrating. Study carrels allow children to have their own small, enclosed space to study and complete their work. Dividers still offer privacy but provide more space. Either one can help your child complete more work, do better academically, and be distracted less often.

15. Use noise-canceling headphones.

Learning at home can be distracting. You don't want your child to miss parts of lessons and information shared through audio. Headphones are a great way to block outside distractions and tune into the lesson.

Noise-canceling headphones eliminate background noise and make it easier to hear. In a recent study, 41% of participants reported using headphones for video teleconferencing (Naddeo, Califano, and Fiorillo, 2021).

Bluetooth and hard-wired options are available. Some Bluetooth models can go for 20 to 30 hours on a single charge, which is more than enough for multiple school days. Many models also allow you to adjust the background noise level. That way, if your child is uncomfortable with active noise being totally canceled, you can adjust the levels to their preference.

Another option are headphones with an integrated mic. Many already have a built-in microphone that can greatly enhance voice quality. Headphones will give you the best sound quality. They also help eliminate echoes that may occur during live lessons.

While your child is using headphones, check in with them from time to time to ensure that they're actually listening to the teacher or educational material. Some children may appear to be attending when in fact they're playing a game or listening to music.

Some children may listen to music on their headphones while they complete independent homework. This can be helpful and even a motivator to finish. However, children shouldn't listen to music while studying.

16. Experiment to determine what screen view works best.

Check in with your child and observe what they see during remote learning. Do they see only the teacher? Do they see the teacher mixed in with the other students? What view is best for them?

Children may be overstimulated with all of the information and views of others on the screen. If there is an option to "pin" the teacher, that could help your child focus. Pinning means the teacher's video feed is the most prominently displayed, and your child may see only a few of their classmates. Even when other students are talking, the teacher is still front and center, similar to the in-person classroom experience. Other children may prefer seeing many of their classmates.

Platforms may have different options. Experiment with small and larger gallery views as well as placement on the screen. Some platforms allow you to split the screen so that you can have the teacher/classmates video on half of the screen or monitor and the instructional materials on the other half.

If your learning platform allows, remove all video feeds and allow your child to listen only to the teacher while looking at lesson content. Try different approaches. Your child may respond better to different views depending on the teacher or subject matter.

17. Practice classroom etiquette during live sessions.

Manners are important. During remote learning, encourage your child to behave as if they were in the brick-and-mortar classroom.

Have your child follow these tips for live lessons:

- Use the mute feature. If the teacher doesn't do this automatically, be sure to mute. That way, no one will hear your home's background noises and your child won't unintentionally interrupt the class.

- Use the chat feature only when directed. Sometimes children may engage in chats that could take away from the instruction. Save chat for when teachers ask students to answer questions or participate in the lesson.

- Actively participate by having the camera on. Video participation allows for an interactive classroom experience and helps build connections between the teacher and students. However, some children may be uncomfortable or fearful of being on video. For example, some become extremely self-conscious when they see themselves on video. Others are concerned that a classmate may unnecessarily pin their video or record their image. Discuss these concerns with your child and the teacher and come to an agreement about the use of video.

- Let others know if you need to step away. Children should let their teacher know via a chat or message if they temporarily leave their workspace. This allows the teacher to know about the status of each student.

18. Ask the teacher to keep everyone on mute and turn off chat.

This tip may not apply to all live sessions, but it's good to keep in mind. Similar to the classroom etiquette tips, this one is related to the classroom environment and how the teacher interacts with students online.

When teachers are focused on the lesson and excited about teaching their students, they sometimes unintentionally overlook areas in the virtual environment.

So encourage your child to speak up and request that your teacher keep everyone on mute if students are interrupting class or there's a lot of noise in the background. Similarly, the teacher needs to know if some children are using the chat feature at an inappropriate time or using it for side discussions.

These friendly reminders to teachers could be a good strategy if students are unnecessarily interrupting class by making noise or engaging in irrelevant chats. When adjustments are made, all children are exposed to the same improved learning environment.

19. Use a blurred or virtual background if you don't want to show your child's background.

Virtual backgrounds allow children to display an image as their background during online instruction. It replaces what's in your child's actual background with the image they select.

You can design your own virtual background with any image that you have rights to or a readily made background.

In general, students should avoid using virtual backgrounds that can be distracting or offensive to the class. Avoid using virtual backgrounds that distort the child's image or makes them appear to have a floating head. Some backgrounds might even be against school policy.

Virtual or blurred backgrounds can be helpful when the real background is cluttered or busy, or if there are privacy concerns. Students and parents may feel uncomfortable letting the classroom into their home. If students are concerned about using their real background, they should talk to their teacher and ask to use a virtual or blurred background.

Virtual backgrounds can also be fun! On special occasions, such as class celebrations and class time related to projects, virtual backgrounds give your child the chance to show off their personality, skills, and creativity. Children may even use apps to design their own virtual background.

20. Use a quiet keyboard and mouse if your child is sensitive to noise.

Keyboarding makes a lot more noise than writing, as you can hear the sound of each letter strike. When you're typing, plastic sliders underneath each key press down on a spring, closing an electrical circuit and activating the corresponding key input. This noise disrupts some students' thinking and can result in stress and anxiety. If there are others nearby, it can be an annoyance to them too. If the sound of the keyboard and mouse bothers your child, there are other options.

A quiet keyboard and mouse can be helpful. These devices are comfortable and quiet. Functionally, a traditional keyboard and mouse work the same way, but the silent versions are easier to type and click.

If you don't want to invest in a quiet keyboard and mouse but feel your child needs quieter tools for remote learning, it's relatively easy to mitigate at least some of the sounds. Silent switches dampen the noise of the plastic parts inside the mechanical housing of a regular keyboard and make it quieter. O-rings are another option. These are tiny rings of silicone, originally intended for sealing gaskets, that you can place around the stem of a key to prevent the sound of it hitting the plate. This option makes a keyboard considerably quieter.

21. Complete all work for the day.

Encourage your child to avoid procrastination and complete all work for the day. Although this may seem like common sense and simple guidance, the remote learning environment has an added component of accountability that you and your child are responsible for at home. Have them get in the habit of completing assigned work by the end of the school day or shortly after. Encourage them to not let work pile up for later.

If your child has regularly scheduled classes or follows a bell schedule, they'll probably need to complete work for each of those subjects during online class. Follow up with your child to ensure they're completing their work.

It becomes more challenging if your student has asynchronous classes or simply has a list of requirements they need to meet for the week. Work with your child to plan what they need to accomplish each day to meet these requirements and stick to this plan.

Despite being engaged in remote learning for hours during the day, your child may have homework they need to do outside class. Establish a regular homework routine, at the same time each day, to ensure all work is completed. Getting it done each day reduces the stress of work piling up and gives your child a sense of accomplishment.

However, going to school at home all day and then facing homework in the same environment can take an emotional toll. In the next chapter, we'll discuss emotional considerations of remote learning.

8 EMOTIONAL CONSIDERATIONS

The third key area for eLearning success looks at emotions. Think about your child's emotional state and needs. How is eLearning impacting them? What can you do to help?

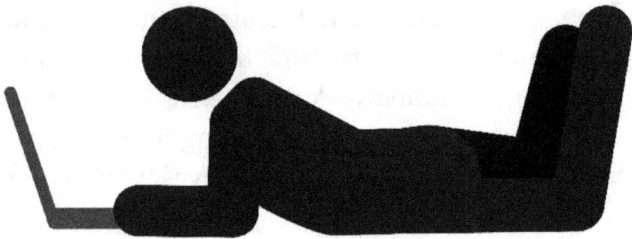

1. Encourage your child to be involved in their learning (personalize the learning).

Children spend a significant amount of their time in the classroom setting each day. What can be done to support them? Encourage your child to be involved in the educational process.

The following strategies can help your child personalize the learning experience:

- Work together to design the space.
- Pick your school materials together.
- Allow your child to personalize or decorate their learning materials and space. For example, they can hang up artwork and inspirational quotes or include a decoration or item that motivates them.
- When presented with work from multiple classes, give your child an opportunity to decide which one they want to tackle first.
- Work with your child to create a schedule.
- Take an interest in your child's education. Ask them what they're learning. Have them to show you what's going on in their classrooms. Ask them to teach you how to navigate their learning platform.

Families that show an interest in learning and encourage their child to be an active learner have children who are more likely to thrive in school (Tan, Lyu, & Peng, 2020).

2. Teach and encourage your child to self-advocate.

What does it mean to self-advocate and why is it important?

Self-advocacy includes:

- Speaking up for yourself
- Making your own decisions about something in your own life
- Learning how to get information so that you can understand what you need and what's important to you
- Finding out who will support you
- Knowing your rights
- Problem-solving
- Reaching out to others when you need help

Self-advocacy is important for your child. It gives them the knowledge they need to succeed and participate in decisions being made about their life.

First, children need to be aware of what they need. If they're struggling in an area (like following along during live instruction, taking notes, or completing homework), they may need to reach out to caregivers or teachers for help. It's also up to the child to let caregivers and teachers know that the strategies are working.

The child also may need to remind caregivers and teachers what they need for continued success. This is especially true for older children who have Individual Education Plans (IEP) or other learning plans. They need to self-advocate to ensure they receive the agreed upon accommodations. This will help them succeed and get comfortable speaking up about their needs.

Talk to your child about their learning. What strengths do they identify? What challenges are they having? How can they recognize what help they need? How can they learn to follow through with asking for help?

Ways children can ask for help include:

During live instruction: "Excuse me, (insert teacher or parent name). I don't understand. Please help me."

Your child can speak up during breaks, when the teacher asks the class if everyone is understanding, or when there's an option on the learning platform to raise their hand or submit a question.

Through email communication: Teach your child how to use the subject line, address the email, and be specific about their problem. Include a screen shot or video clip if needed. Timing is crucial when it comes to getting help, so send the email as soon as the class is over.

3. Acknowledge that remote learning is temporary (if it is).

Some children are thriving in an eLearning environment. They're in a daily routine, are completing work, and enjoy interacting with teachers and peers in a remote setting.

Some children may be doing okay but miss being in the traditional classroom setting.

Others may be struggling with many or all aspects of remote learning. It's a challenging time, and the virtual environment is significantly different from the in-person setting.

Let your child know that eLearning is a temporary situation only if that's the truth. The decision to participate in eLearning is a personal one, made by each family if the school district offers options. Some families are choosing to keep their children at home due to family members' significant health concerns and the need to reduce the risk of exposure to illness.

Talk openly with your child about your situation, particularly if you can choose remote learning, hybrid learning, or in-person class. Don't make promises you can't keep if the school hasn't decided when students will return to the in-person setting. Similarly, don't tell your child that they'll return to the in-person classroom if you intend to keep them home or if you aren't sure when they'll go back. This will only disappoint them and cause them to not trust you.

If you have a concern about your child's mental health as a result of eLearning, talk to them. Look for negative changes in behavior. Have they been crying more often, talking back more, or starting arguments? Listen to what they have to say about the situation. If they express thoughts of wanting to hurt themself or others, immediately reach out to your doctor for help.

4. Help your child build a social network.

Human beings are social by nature. Social connection and being a part of a group are basic needs. Even children who prefer to be alone benefit from regular social interaction.

During remote learning, children typically have some experiences with their peers. In this environment, they can collaborate and learn together. However, children need peer interaction beyond the classroom.

Virtual groups are a good way for children to connect. These can be groups on various social media platforms, group texts, or group video calls. Online gaming activities are another way to connect through a common interest, especially if the children chat online while they play. But monitor your child's online social networks because they may sometimes provide a false sense of connectedness.

Some families have permitted their children to be in physical contact with close friends during the pandemic. Also any extracurricular activity outside the home provides a way for children to socialize.

The benefits of socialization:

- It's good for mental health. It can make you feel happy.

- It promotes a sense of safety, belonging, and security.

- It allows you to develop a relationship, which enables you to confide in someone and them to confide in you.

5. Teach your child to engage in self-care activities.

In the eLearning environment, your child will likely spend at least 25 hours per week in front of the screen. But they're not designed to sit in front of a computer for hours on end. While learning addresses children's cognitive needs, it's important for them to get their other needs (physical, emotional, social, belongingness, and love) met. This will help them be more successful in the classroom and improve their well-being.

Ideas for Self-Care Activities

- Singing
- Gardening
- Reading a book or magazine
- Playing a game
- Sewing
- Making a craft
- Watching funny videos
- Calling friends or family
- Playing with a pet
- Journaling
- Writing poetry
- Drawing
- Taking a nap
- Yoga
- Meditation
- Exercise
- Taking a walk
- Fishing
- Biking
- Hiking
- Swimming
- Playing
- Puzzles

- Building a fort
- Making silly videos
- Taking funny photos
- Doing nails
- Doing hair
- Prayer
- Planning an activity or event

What are other ideas you have for self-care?

6. Help your child build a growth mindset.

Your mindset is a collection of thoughts and beliefs that affect how you make decisions and view the world. If you have a fixed mindset, you tend to resist the possibility of growth and change. You focus on what's familiar and stay in your comfort zone and defined boundaries.

Stanford psychologist Carol Dweck (2006) coined the phrase "growth mindset." Growth mindset is the tendency to believe you can grow and change through experience. If you have a growth mindset, you have an open mind and focus on how you can grow through experiences and intentional effort. You embrace challenges.

How to build a growth mindset:
- View challenges as opportunities.
- Try different learning tactics. Don't give up!
- Replace the word *failing* with the word *learning*.
- View criticism as positive.

Benefits of a growth mindset:
- Improves brain development across tasks
- Leads to better relationships
- Lowers anxiety, stress, and depression
- Increases goal-setting
- Makes you more comfortable with taking personal risks

Building a growth mindset takes persistence and time. But the benefits are worth it, and it will prepare your child to be successful as an adult. Applying a growth mindset also improves motivation. In the next chapter, we'll discuss motivational strategies for the eLearning environment.

9 MOTIVATIONAL STRATEGIES

Key area number four for a successful learning environment involves motivational strategies. In this section, let's discuss what you can do to keep your child motivated and engaged in online schooling. How can you give your child an extra push?

1. Offer a choice when possible.

We're all motivated by needs. When children don't comply, one possible reason is that a need isn't being met. According to Maslow's (1943) five-tier hierarchy of needs, we all have a series of needs, and our most basic needs must be satisfied before we can focus on needs that are higher in the hierarchy.

Our basic needs are:

- Physiological (food, clothing, water, rest, and shelter)
- Safety (security)

These must be met before our other needs are met. They are:

- Psychological, which include belongingness and love needs (friendship, family, sense of connection)
- Esteem (self-esteem, recognition, respect)

At the top of the hierarchy is the need for self-actualization, or achieving one's full potential.

Children don't enjoy constantly being told what to do. No one does! Children may sometimes be resistant or even refuse to follow through on a task. That's where the power of choice comes in. When you provide a choice, it gives your child a sense of control. You really have the control, though, because you decide which options to give. The child, however, will feel they have power, as they're choosing which task or activity they'll do.

Let's say your child doesn't want to complete their schoolwork because they want to socialize with a friend. Explain that their behavior won't get them what they want. Think about what need they're trying to meet. Suggest an alternative way and ask for their input. If they still don't comply, then offer a choice.

For example, say, "You can do your math homework first or your science project before you FaceTime your friend." That's it. If necessary, point out that they didn't choose to comply at first even when asked for their input, so they now have a choice to make

Children can get overwhelmed if there are too many choices to begin with. So providing specific options can help reduce stress and help your child focus.

2. Have your child check off tasks as they go for a sense of accomplishment.

Lists come in a variety of forms, and they're important. They capture everything your child needs to get done in one place so they don't forget. Prioritizing the tasks on the list ensures that your child pays attention to what needs to be done first and what can wait. When your child crosses off tasks as they're completed, they get a sense of accomplishment.

Try one or more of the following methods until you find one that works.

- Some children simply need to focus on getting through the day. So print out a daily or weekly class schedule and tape it up in your child's workspace. Cross off each class as it's finished for the day.

- Make a list of daily homework that needs to be completed. Check off each assignment when finished.

- Make a list of projects that need to be done for the week and prioritize them. Mark them as they're completed.

- Use a small notebook dedicated to lists so you can track assignments, projects, and other school-related activities all in one place. This could be a good strategy for giving older children an opportunity to reflect on their lists and make future adjustments.

Checking off activities as they're completed provides satisfaction and a good visual of all of the hard work your student accomplished. Some get excited about tearing the list up and tossing it out when they're finished.

3. Break projects into smaller tasks.

Projects and large assignments can be overwhelming for children of all ages. With so much to do, it can be difficult to figure out where to start. They can successfully complete a project by breaking it down into steps that are more manageable.

How to break a project down into smaller tasks:

1. Read through the entire instructions with your child to ensure they understand the goal of the assignment or project and what's required.
2. Have them follow up with the teacher to clarify anything that's unclear.
3. Make sure your child has all the materials or supplies they need.
4. Break the project into small steps and list them out.
5. With the due date in mind, assign a completion date next to each step. Be realistic about how much time each will take, as some steps will take longer than others.
6. Cross off the steps as they're completed.
7. If your child falls behind, look at the steps ahead to see where adjustments can be made to make up time.
8. Encourage your child to ask for help along the way as needed.
9. Before submitting the assignment, reread the instructions and check the project to ensure all parts are completed. If the teacher provided a rubric, this is a good time to make sure your child met all the requirements.

These steps will help ensure that the project was well thought out and organized. It will likely give your child confidence to complete future projects. Model this process a few times for your child. Eventually, they'll do these steps on their own.

4. Collaborate with your child to develop rewards for effort.

Schoolwork can be challenging. Some children are intrinsically motivated. They have an internal desire to do well and follow through. Children who are interested in or enjoy the challenge of schoolwork are intrinsically motivated to succeed. They likely don't need to be rewarded for effort, but it doesn't hurt to reward them occasionally to acknowledge a job well done.

On the other hand, some children are extrinsically motivated. That is, external factors help get them to complete tasks. Rewards are helpful for these children. I'm not talking about bribing. Extrinsically motivated children likely work to earn something. For example, if they finish their homework, they can watch TV. If they pay attention during math class, they can have extra time outside. Another reward can be doing something they enjoy that doesn't involve screen time. It is optimistic to note that both intrinsic motivation and well-internalized forms of extrinsic motivation predict positive outcomes in children in school and are enhanced by supports for students' basic psychological needs for competence, relatedness, and autonomy (Ryan & Deci, 2020).

Find out what rewards your child would like to earn. They don't need to cost money. The examples above cost nothing. But for this to work, your child needs to be interested in the reward.

I want to make a note about screen time. Since your child is on the computer for a significant time each day, don't extend screen time as a reward. If you allow 30 minutes of screen time outside school per day, then your child's reward for doing their work is 30 minutes, not 30 minutes of additional screen time.

All children are different. You may have one child who's intrinsically motivated and another who's extrinsically motivated. It's a balancing act. Both types may enjoy attending school, but the one who's extrinsically motivated needs a little push to get it done.

5. Find your child's motivation.

If your child isn't motivated, maybe they're anxious about school. The work may be too hard or not challenging enough, or your child may not feel confident about school. What basic needs aren't being met?

Talk to your child. What's stopping them? What motivates them to do well? You may think you have an idea, but until you talk to them, you can't be certain. Motivation is the reason behind behavior.

How can you encourage motivation to learn?

- Observe your child to find out where their interests lie and tie them back to schooling. Is there a way to tie their interests into a class assignment?

- Focus on learning over performance. Celebrate completion of big and small tasks. When the focus is taken away from grades, your child will learn to enjoy accomplishing tasks, which increases motivation.

- Find ways to link interests with skills you want your child to develop. For example, if they're really excited about Bigfoot but don't like to read, find a book about Bigfoot that you can read together to work on developing reading skills.

- Ask your child about an assignment they're working on and have them explain how they solved a problem or answered a question.

If you tried all of the strategies but still have difficulty motivating your child to participate in school or complete work, reach out to the school for support. The next section, covers the importance of home-school communication.

10 HOME-SCHOOL COMMUNICATION

Key area number five for a successful learning environment is good home-school communication.

How can you begin to work with or work better with your child's school?

1. Use school resources for support.

Schools are designed to help educate students and to prepare them for life outside the classroom. Teachers want your child to be successful. Whenever you need support for remote learning, turn to your school first.

Your child's school may or may not have all of these resources, but the following list is a good place to start.

- **Resources provided by your child's teacher:** This includes books, handouts, notes, videos, apps, and all instructional materials. Check in with the teacher if you're missing something or need more (like extra practice worksheets or additional videos). Stay connected with homeroom teachers for information about what's going on in the classroom and school-related events. Check your email regularly. Many teachers send parents log-on instructions for applications, websites, and learning goals.

- **Parent handbook:** Most schools have a handbook for parents that includes information on what resources the school has available and how to access them.

- **School learning platform:** The online learning platform is where your child logs on and attends school. Learn about the entire platform. Some schools require more than one. Some let you have separate accounts that link to your child's account. This allows you to monitor grades, assignments, and the curriculum.

- **Student support services:** These include guidance services, mental health support, college and career planning, and exceptional student services. If your child is struggling with peer relationships, anxiety, or depression, contact the school to connect with the school counselor, including skills groups or counseling that may be available. If your child is struggling academically, including with speech and language concerns, talk to the teacher and school administrator about next steps. These may include interventions and further evaluation to determine the best academic supports for your child. Some children may be eligible for one-to-one support or have access to a classroom aide. If your high school student is struggling with career or college options, ask about college and career planning.

- **School newsletter:** Those on the school's website or emailed to you typically share information about learning activities and how you can help your child. Subscribe to it if given the option.

- **School Facebook groups for parents:** These are typically started by parents, who can provide valuable support and resources to each other, typically in a timely manner.

- **School presence on social media:** Your child's school may use Instagram, Twitter, YouTube, TikTok, or another platform to share important school events and information.

- **School website:** Check it regularly for updates. You may learn about resources that could help your child.

Many outside resources are also available. Going down this path can be overwhelming, so tap into all school resources first.

2. Check with the teacher to see if copies of notes and materials are available.

Children may have difficulty navigating all their class information on the learning platform. If they need help locating it, encourage them to reach out to the teacher to ask. If your child is younger, you may need to do this for them.

Are all class notes and materials for the week or semester located in one place on the learning platform? Does your child need to access multiple sites and folders? Make sure they know where to find all the materials. Make a list of all of the learning applications and websites they need and tape it at your child's learning station.

Additionally, if your child needs notes about a particular subject matter, ask the teacher if they're available. Also ask for other materials to support your child as needed. For example, there may be additional websites, books, and videos that enhance your child's learning. Some children may struggle with reading or need the material reinforced in another manner. Textbooks and novels in audio format are another great way to gain access to and learn the material.

If your child is absent from school, find out how they can get notes and materials. Assignments may be readily available on the learning platform, and a trusted classmate can also fill your child in on what they missed. Best practice is to always check in with the teacher. At times, additional or different material may have been covered than what was originally planned. This method of follow-up is also a form of self-advocacy and a way for your child to demonstrate to their teacher that they're responsible.

3. Parent-teacher conferences and parent-teacher-student conferences.

Parent-teacher conferences that involve the student's caregiver and teacher, as well as parent-teacher-student conferences that include the student's caregiver, teacher, and the student, are ways to increase home-school communication. These conferences help you stay in touch with the school, understand expectations, and get to know the teacher. It provides you with the opportunity to openly discuss your child's progress in school.

During these conferences, it's a good idea to give the teacher a heads-up about anything that may be going on at home that could be impacting your child's performance in school. For example, caregivers' and siblings' schedules, new pets and babies, job loss, and medical issues may all impact your child. When children are included in these conferences, it's an opportunity for them to assume responsibility for their education, discuss concerns, and ask questions. Conferences are a safe environment where the parent and child are supported. This leads to higher engagement and better school performance.

Schools typically offer conferences in the middle of the first semester or when report cards are released. But what if your child is really struggling, and it's not conference time yet? Don't wait. Reach out to the teacher and ask for a meeting to discuss your child's progress. This can help resolve issues early and obtain the support your child needs. You can also ask what you can do to help at home.

4. Ask for help from the teacher or school staff if needed.

Keep the lines of communication with the school open. Your main communication is typically through your child's teachers. They're responsible for each child in their class. Teachers want your child to attend school and make progress, so if your child isn't present or is struggling, they're more than likely the first ones willing to help.

The eLearning environment can be a challenge to navigate at times. Information is in many places. Sometimes it may be a hard to access the correct information. Start with your child's teacher if you have a question about the class or need clarification about assignments and other requirements. Let the teacher know if you're struggling with technology or your internet connection. Be open about your struggles so they can understand the situation. If your child isn't logging in for eLearning due to technical difficulties, family circumstances, illnesses, or other challenges, let teachers know so they can help find a solution. If teachers are kept in the dark, they won't be able to help. If it's a technology challenge and you can't communicate through email or the learning platform, call the school or reach out to another parent who can help you.

What's the best way to contact your child's teachers? If they didn't share this information in the materials you have, locate the contact information you can find and send a short message asking for the best way to communicate. While many teachers prefer emails or conversations through a messaging system on the learning platform, some are open to phone calls and texts. Others may require a more formal approach, such as a scheduled meeting.

If it's not an urgent matter, give your child's teacher 24 hours before following up. Check to ensure your message went through. Teachers may receive many messages. Plus, they're also teaching class and grading assignments, so it can take some time for them to respond. In the rare event your child's teacher isn't responsive, reach out to a school administrator (principal, vice principal, administrative assistant) so they can determine the best action to take.

In general, home-school communication is vital to your child's success. It can lead to improved academic achievement, a more confident child, better relationships, and improved school attendance and work completion. Take time to learn how to navigate the school and all the available resources. Establish a working relationship with the teacher, as you both desire the best for your child.

In the next section, we discuss your role as a parent during remote learning

11 CAREGIVER'S ROLE

Key area number six for a successful learning environment is the caregiver's role. You play an important part in getting your eLearner on the right track. What do you need to do for yourself and your child?

1. Engage in daily self-care activities.

Are you feeling tired, exhausted, overwhelmed, or confused? You're constantly taking care of everyone and everything in the home. It's already emotionally, mentally, and physically draining. When remote learning is added to the mix, it can push you over the edge.

Stop! Give yourself a pat on the back and acknowledge ALL that you've done. Parenting is hard work without the added responsibility of remote learning. You're doing an amazing job! It may not feel that way at times, but if you're trying and are there for your child when you can be, that's what counts. In general, we're too hard on ourselves because we want the best for our child. Take a deep breath. Everything will be okay. Let's focus on you for a moment and what you can do to help yourself.

What is self-care and why is it important?

Self-care consists of activities and behaviors that we do to take care of ourselves and improve our overall health, which then, in turn, allows us to take better care of others. Self-care focuses on all aspects of ourselves, including physical, mental, emotional, cognitive, and social health. Those who engage in self-care activities are more likely to have improved overall well-being and lower healthcare costs (Riegel, Dunbar, Fitzsimons, Freedland, Lee, Middleton, Stromber, Vellone, Webber, & Jaarsma, 2019).

Take care of yourself before you take care of others.

No, this is not selfish, and I'm not suggesting that you ignore your caretaking responsibilities. But even if it's only five minutes, you need time for yourself. You'll be in a better state of mind and, more importantly, in a better position to take care of others.

For example, if you need a few extra minutes in the morning to get yourself together or finish your coffee, take time to do that. You'll feel more relaxed and ready to go. Likewise, if you're angry or irritated with something else going on in your life, stop, step away, and regroup.

If you're struggling with guilt, think about this for a moment. Whenever people are on an airplane, the flight attendant instructs adults to put on their masks first before putting on their child's mask. You need to protect yourself before you can effectively help someone else.

As a longer-term strategy, engage in regular self-care activities, such as exercise, getting plenty of sleep, and eating healthy. Make time to do something each week that brings you joy. Put it on your calendar.

Self-care also goes beyond the activities that we do to take care of ourselves, such as exercise, baths, sports, skin care routines, and massages. These are all important. But in order to promote deeper self-care, try these activities:

- Cry
- Feel emotions (yes, this can be frightening)
- Set boundaries
- Engage in difficult conversations to resolve problems and move forward
- Establish and follow a sleep routine
- Think positively
- Forgive others
- Seek counseling as needed to heal from trauma and unresolved childhood issues

2. Think about the complexity of learning.

Learning is not simply sitting down in front of the computer and attending class. Think about the complexity of learning. Your child needs a variety of support—academic, technological, psychological, and environmental.

The eLearning environment is demanding. Your home is also your classroom. Your child is relying on you for various supports.

- **Academic:** They need you to help with their homework and to navigate the academic environment.

- **Technological:** They're relying on you to make sure they have all the devices and equipment they need, the internet is set up, and they can access all their classes. They need help troubleshooting when things don't go as planned.

- **Psychological:** Children also rely on you for psychological support. Encourage your child throughout eLearning and take time to listen to their concerns. Help them manage their feelings and frustrations.

- **Environmental (structure):** Your child depends on you for structure. Some may say they don't like structure, but they strive when a structured environment is provided. It helps them know what to do and what's expected of them.

Do you ever wonder why you're so tired? Remote learning requires all of the above supports. Acknowledging all that goes into it can put the learning process into perspective. Tackle one area at a time.

3. Identify barriers.

As you've probably discovered, eLearning doesn't run smoothly 100% of the time. If your child appears frustrated or work isn't getting completed, find out why. Is it technology issues, environmental issues, or something related to your child's health or well-being?

Talk to your child. Check in with their mental and physical condition, as these can have an effect on learning. Low blood sugar can reduce concentration. A humid environment can cause sluggishness. If it's too hot or cold in the learning environment, your child could be distracted. If they're in pain or aren't feeling good, they won't perform at their best.

Pay attention to the environment as discussed earlier in this book. Recheck it for barriers to learning. For example, is the internet not working? Does your child's eLearning workspace need to be adjusted?

Perhaps it's fear or a lack of confidence. Does your child lack confidence in their skills related to a particular subject? Are they worried they're not learning as quickly or are smart as others? Fear could be a factor. Is your child fearful of failing? Do they have a fear of change as it relates to their education or being in a remote environment? Identifying barriers are half the battle.

Now, do what it takes to resolve it. This may mean new equipment, adjustments to the learning space, a change in eating and sleeping routines, or reaching out to others who can help. Tackle the barriers as soon as you can, as some issues may have a cumulative effect and be more challenging to fix in the future, resulting in even more frustration for you and your child.

4. Be positive.

Think positively, not negatively. Positive thinking is an emotional thought process and mental attitude that focuses on the good. It's a mindset that involves anticipating that good things will happen. With practice, positive thinking can become a habit over time and reduce negative thoughts that so often automatically pop into our minds.

No one has a positive attitude 100% of the time, and that's okay. Acknowledge it and accept it. One way to improve positive thinking is to replace every negative thought that comes into your mind with two or three positive thoughts or alternatives. Even if you don't truly believe these positive thoughts, be open to exploring them.

Your child looks up to you as a role model. They receive cues from you as to how to behave. If you talk negatively about remote learning, your child will pick up on these comments. It won't impact their schoolwork and remote school experience in a favorable manner.

Remote learning may certainly not be ideal for many children, but try to do your best given the circumstances. When you and your child encountered and overcame challenges in the remote learning environment, what did you both learn? How did the challenge help you? How can it help you or others in the future?

Negative thinking can result in poor mood, memory problems, and slow reaction time. But positive thinking has health benefits. It can also lead to increased productivity in the remote learning environment, enhanced creativity, improved focus, better problem-solving skills, and good mental health.

After all, it's more fun to be around others who are generally positive.

5. Be consistent.

Consistency is a major key to success in an eLearning environment.

What is consistency? It's doing something repeatedly at regular intervals. It helps build regular momentum and habits, and it's necessary for continued academic achievement. Consistency is also one of the major components of success when it comes to exercising, dieting, weight loss, and achieving goals in general.

Consistency with morning and evening routines is important for success. For example, stick to a regular morning routine and make sure your child is ready to go each morning (getting dressed, eating breakfast, brushing teeth, and being at the learning space by 8:30 a.m.). Check regularly to ensure your child is attending all classes every day.

You'll need to make sure that your child's learning environment is set up and that they're engaging in class and completing assignments. Establish a regular evening routine so that your child goes to bed around the same time each night.

Involve your children in the creation of routines. For example, at the beginning of each week, you can compile a lunch menu for each school day. It's fun for the students, and it will save your family time.

This is a lot to manage, and it's unrealistic to expect younger children to navigate the remote environment by themselves. So it's up to parents to provide consistency and hold children accountable. It does requires significant time and energy at first, but it will eventually become a habit. It can just be a slow process and take time to get there.

Older children will likely be more independent and pick up the routines quicker. Younger children will also catch on, but they may need more encouragement, modeling, and direct instruction. If your child sees you engaging in consistent, healthy routines, they're likely to follow.

6. Establish work and remote school boundaries.

Boundaries are important, as they set expectations for your behavior and your child's behavior. All caregivers, regardless of whether they work from home, can benefit from establishing work and remote-school boundaries. Boundaries allow you to have some space and freedom to accomplish household tasks, make phone calls, or do remote work. They also allow your child to have space as needed, participate in online learning, and learn how to solve problems independently (or with help from their teacher or classmates). Most importantly, setting boundaries should prevent (or at the very least reduce) times when your child interrupts you.

Work with your child to establish boundaries and set the expectations. For example, you can have a signal for when your child cannot interrupt you during work. If they see a Do Not Disturb sign on your door, they know they'll need to wait to talk to you. If they see you on a phone call, they're expected to not interrupt you. Be proactive. If you know you're going to be on a conference call at a certain time, let them know that morning and write it down for them in their work area so they know not to interrupt. Let your child know what they can do, whom they can reach out to and how for times when you're not available.

Predictability is also important. If you're fortunate enough to have multiple caregivers in the home, you can split the duties during remote learning. Make sure there is some consistency and clearly communicate the schedule to your child. For example, say, "Mommy can help you until 11 a.m. today, and then your grandmother will be available the rest of the day."

It's important to stick to a schedule. Be realistic, though, as emergencies come up and sometimes things change. Be sure to communicate clearly with household members.

7. Ensure the health of your child, physically, emotionally and mentally. Do what's best for you and your family.

Family is one of the most important things in life. Do what's best for you and your family. Adults need to rely on each other for support in meeting their children's needs. It takes a village, and you may need extended family, neighbors, doctors, and other professionals to assist. Do what you can to ensure the health of your child, physically, emotionally, and mentally.

Physical: Make sure your child is safe, and do what you can to make sure their most basic needs of food, clean clothes, and a stable place to live are met.

Emotional: Ask how your child is feeling and talk about it. Some children may be worried about getting sick or infecting others. They may feel responsible if someone in the home lost their job or if adults around them are arguing more often. Acknowledge your child's feelings and assure them that consequences of the pandemic aren't their fault. Discuss how your child can cope with various feelings.

Mental: There has been an increase in depression, anxiety, and loneliness since the pandemic began (Patrick et al., 2020). If your child is struggling in these areas, reach out to your school and pediatrician for resources to support them.

Learning options vary across the country, from full-time online learning, to a hybrid approach, to all in-person school. If you have options, the choices can be overwhelming. If you're struggling with your decision or are feeling guilty, it's okay. Millions of families are making tough choices about education, care-giving, employment, housing, and family responsibilities every day.

When it comes to education, if you have choices, the right option is the one that you've chosen for your family. You've considered the risks and benefits and how different decisions may affect you and your family.

What works well for one family may not work well for another. Remember, you need to meet your family's needs. Even within the same family, some parents have decided to send one child to the in-person environment and keep the other one as a remote learner.

8. Help your child understand the material. Don't teach, and don't do their work.

Help your children understand the material. But don't teach, and don't do the work for them. Granted, this can be easier said than done. As parents, we want to rescue our children. We don't want to see them fail. Your first instinct may be to rush in and complete the work for them because it's easier and quicker and you don't want to hear them complain. Then the work is done, and you don't have to push your child to do it. However, this quick solution is not in your child's best interest. They haven't learned the material, but they have learned that you will rescue them repeatedly, which can lead to learned helplessness.

While it may feel like it, your role as the caregiver is not to replace the teacher. You're there to coach, assist, encourage, and guide your child along the way.

Help them with their work if you can, but don't do it for them. Your child may need to reach out to their teacher. Facilitate this interaction if your child isn't sure how to ask for help. Reassure them that their teacher wants them to be successful. After all, your child wouldn't need to be in school if they had already mastered all of the coursework. If your child is older, there could be a peer who can help your child with the challenging material.

Encourage your child to bring in past knowledge to help them with current assignments. Have them make connections between their current work and events from the real world. They don't make these connections as easily as we do.

Talk to your child each day about their school day.

You can ask:

- What was your favorite thing you learned today?

- What was the hardest?

- What do you have questions about today?

- What was the best thing that happened?

This will help your child reflect on the learning process. When you show an interest in your child's education, you can strengthen your relationship.

9. Do something fun each day!

Life has changed with the pandemic and seems more stressful at times. As a caregiver, you do so much for your child and their education. Learning is important, but if you focus much of your time on fighting with your child to do work or stressing out about how to complete and submit assignments the right way, you'll only end up with more stress and frustration. Unfortunately, many children will no longer enjoy school if these patterns repeat.

Stop. Your child will eventually catch up, meet grade-level expectations, and likely receive instruction in the class they weren't able to take online. Things will get back on track at some point. The education system and instructional practices are continuing to evolve.

Take time each day to do something fun with your family. Shared fun is generally more enjoyable than solitary fun (Reis, O'Keefe, & Lane, 2016). A fun activity doesn't need to cost money or involve hours of planning. It can be anything from playing cards or a board game, doing a craft, learning something new together, cooking, or sharing a hobby with a family member. Brainstorm fun activities and put something on the calendar for each day if possible.

At a minimum, aim to have fun several times each week. If you can't do it every day as a family, that's okay too. We all need time to ourselves, and some fun activities may be solitary, such as reading or practicing an individual skill. If possible, try to engage in a fun activity that doesn't involve screen time.

10. Monitor your child's online activities.

We would like to believe that our children are automatically safe when they engage in remote learning. Schools provide only the learning platforms and tools to participate. It's your responsibility to monitor internet activities. It's also up to parents to teach their children how to use the internet safely and judge the information available to them online (Lepkowska, 2021).

10 Reasons to Monitor Online Activities

1. **Participation in educational activities**: Ensure you child is attending school and completing their required work. Troubleshoot if needed.

2. **Limit screen time:** Your child is already spending hours online for school, so limit free time they spend online.

3. **Online predators:** The internet is the most popular method for online predators to take advantage of children. They may pretend to be your child's friend, so check whom your child is interacting with online.

4. **Cyberbullying:** Children may tease and taunt one another through classroom chats, email, or discussion boards.

5. **Dangerous activities:** If you check on your child's activities, you could stumble upon other children who are in crisis and need help. You may also find conversations about illegal activities that require intervention.

6. **Protect their personal information:** Children need to be educated about what information is and is not appropriate to provide to others.

7. **Identity theft:** There are many phishing emails and schemes designed to obtain information so your identity can be stolen. This can negatively impact your child's future, including their credit.

8. **Monitor their reputation:** Check in on your child's chats to see if they're demonstrating appropriate social skills with friends. Provide coaching.

9. **Viruses:** Viruses can damage operating systems and computers.

10. **Sexting:** Talk to your children about the dangers and long-term consequences of sending sexually suggestive messages and nude pics.

12 SUMMARY

You made it! We covered the six key areas for success in an eLearning environment. Let's review.

1. **Physical environment:** We looked at what the eLearner environment set-up should look like, how it should be organized, and where it should be located. I also gave an overview of materials and devices you'll need.
2. **During eLearning:** Here we focused on what your child should be doing during the learning process each day to maximize success.
3. **Emotional considerations:** We considered how eLearning is impacting your child's emotional state and needs. We discussed what you can do to help and how children can help themselves.
4. **Motivational strategies:** We covered how some children are intrinsically motivated and others may need a little push. That is okay. Find out what motivates your child and tie that into the eLearning process to get things accomplished.
5. **Home-school communication:** These two systems need each other for success. We need to establish and maintain good and regular communication to further the educational progress of our children.
6. **Caregiver's role:** We discussed the importance of your role in the eLearning process. Your role in supporting your child's journey through eLearning and navigating the educational system is critical.

All of these components are important for success.

Six Key Areas for Success in an eLearning Environment

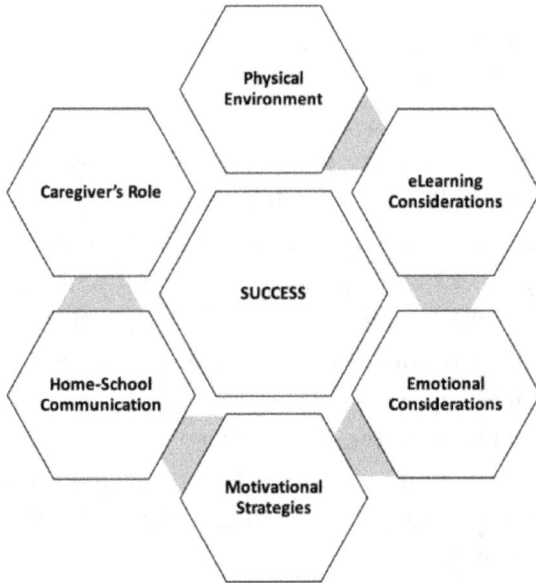

REFERENCES

Andrew, A., Cattan, S., Costa-Dias, M., Farquharson, C., Kraftman, L., Krutikova, S., Phimister, A., Sevilla, A. (2020). *Learning during the lockdown: real-time data on children's experiences during home learning.* The Institute for Fiscal Studies. https://doi.org/ 10.1920/BN.IFS.2020.BN0288

Carrier, L.M., Rosen, L.D., Cheever, N.A., Lim, A.F. (2015). Causes, effects, and practicalities of everyday multitasking. *Developmental Review, 35,* 64-78. https://doi.org/10.1016/j.dr.2014.12.005.

Castellucci, H., Arezes, P., & Molenbroek, J. (2015). Equations for defining the mismatch between students and school furniture: A systematic review. *International Journal of Industrial Ergonomics, 48,* 117-126. https://www.sciencedirect.com/science/article/abs/pii/S01698 14115000670

Chang, S.L., & Ley, K. (2006). A learning strategy to compensate for cognitive overload in online learning: Learner use of printed online materials. *Journal of Interactive Online Learning, 5*(1), 104-117.

Dabrowiecki, A., Villalobos, A., & Krupinski, E. A. (2020). *Blue light filtering glasses and computer vision syndrome: a pilot study.* Proc. SPIE 11316, Medical Imaging 2020: Image Perception, Observer Performance, and Technology Assessment, 1131609. https://doi.org/10.1117/12.2547776

Dweck, C.S. (2006). *Mindset: The new psychology of success. How we can learn to fulfill our potential.* Random House.

Kirby, T. (2020). *The effect of fidget spinners on attention and anxiety in typically developing children.* [Thesis]. Washburn University. https://wuir.washburn.edu/handle/10425/2500

Lepkowska, D. (2021). Internet safety: Teaching children to keep themselves safe. *British Journal of Child Health, 1*(6). https://doi.org/10.12968/chhe.2020.1.6.265

Maslow, A.H. (1943). A theory of human motivation. *Psychological Review, 50*(4), 370–96. https://doi.org/ 10.1037/h0054346

Naddeo, A., Califano, R., and Fiorillo, I. (2021). Identifying factors that influenced wellbeing and learning effectiveness during the sudden transition into eLearning due to the COVID-19 lockdown. *Work, 68*(1), 45-67. https://doi.org/10.3233/WOR-203358

National Institutes of Health (NIH). (n.d.). *Nutrient recommendations: dietary reference intakes (DRI).* https://ods.od.nih.gov/HealthInformation/Dietary_Reference_Intakes.aspx

Patrick, S.W., Henkhaus, L.E., Zickafooose, J.S., Lovell, K., Halvorson, A., Loch, S., Letterie, M., Davis, M.M. (2020). Well-being of parents and children during the COVID-19 pandemic: A national survey. *Pediatrics, 146*(4), e2020016824. https://doi.org/10.1542/peds.2020-016824

Reis, H.T., O'Keefe, S.D., & Lane, R.D. (2016). Fun is more fun when others are involved. The Journal of Positive Psychology, 12:6, 547-557. https://doi.org/ 10.1080/17439760.2016.1221123

Riegel, B., Dunbar, S.B., Fitzsimons, D., Freedland, K.E., Lee, C.S.,

Middleton, S., Stromberg, A., Vellone, E., Webber, D.E., & Jaarsma, T. (2019). Self-care research: Where are we now? Where are we going? *International Journal of Nursing Studies*, 22, 31. https://doi.org/10.1016/j.ijnurstu.2019.103402.

Rosen, L.D., Carrier, L.M., & Cheever, N.A (2013). Facebook and texting made me do it: Media-induced task-switching while studying. *Computers in Human Behavior*, 29(3), 948-958. https://doi.org/10.1016/j.chb.2012.12.001.

Ryan, R.M., Deci, E.L. (2020). Intrinsic and extrinsic motivation from a self-determination theory perspective: Definitions, theory, practices, and future directions. *Contemporary Educational Psychology*, 61, 101860, ISSN 0361-476X. https://doi.org/10.1016/j.cedpsych.2020.101860.

Sieber, J. E. (2005). Misconceptions and realities about teaching online. *Science and Engineering Ethics*, 11(3), 329-340. https://doi.org/10.1007/s11948-005-0002-7

Spagnola, M., & Fiese, B.H. (2007). Family routines and rituals: A context for development in the lives of young children. *Infants & Young Children*, 20(4): 284-299.

Tan, C.Y., Lyu, Meiyan, & Peng, B. (2020). Academic benefits from parental involvement are stratified by parental socioeconomic status: A meta-analysis. *Parenting*, 20(4), 241-287. https://doi.org/ 10.1080/15295192.2019.1694836

Wilson, V.E., Peper, E. (2004). The effects of upright and slumped postures on the recall of positive and negative thoughts. *Applied Psychophysiological Biofeedback*, 29, 189–195. https://doi.org/10.1023/B:APBI.0000039057.32963.34

ABOUT THE AUTHOR

Carrie Champ Morera, PsyD, BC-TMH, LPC, NCSP, LP

Dr. Champ Morera is a board-certified telemental health professional, licensed professional counselor, nationally certified school psychologist, and licensed psychologist. She has over 20 years of experience in the education and behavioral health fields, specializing in working with children and adolescents. She has worked in a variety of settings, including public schools, private residential schools, outpatient settings, private practice, telehealth, and a psychological test publishing company.